MORE RAVES FOR LAST SEASON'S EDITION

If all this talk about kilowatts and landfills sounds a little grim, it needn't be. In San Francisco the Evergreen Alliance has published a light-hearted paperback... —LOS ANGELES TIMES

A Green Christmas Primer of tips...it's easy being green. —FLAIR

A Good informative book... A reminder that Christmas doesn't need to be purchased to be merry. —BUZZWORM

For your ecologically inclined friends who will be very impressed you found it. —COURIER-GAZETTE, ROCKLAND, MAINE

Chockfull of ideas that make celebrating the Holidays more fun, and more in the spirit of the Holiday. — NATURE SOCIETY NEWS

...offers hundreds of ways to make the earth cleaner and greener. —PARENT

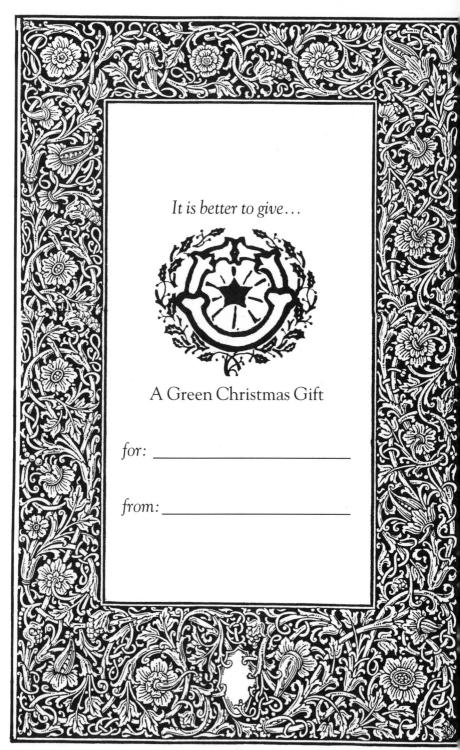

It is better to give…

A Green Christmas Gift

for: _____

from: _____

THE NEW GREEN CHRISTMAS

HOW TO MAKE THIS AND EVERY HOLIDAY AN ENVIRONMENTAL CELEBRATION

BY THE EVERGREEN ALLIANCE

HALO BOOKS
SAN FRANCISCO, CALIFORNIA

THIS BOOK IS PRINTED ON RECYCLED PAPER.

Published by:

HALO BOOKS
P.O. Box 2529, San Francisco, CA

Copyright © 1991 by Halo Books

Created by The Evergreen Alliance

Cover by Susan Larson

Printed in the United States of America

Library of Congress Cataloging-in-Publication Data
Available Upon Request

HALO BOOKS
P.O. Box 2529, San Francisco, CA 94126
For Ordering Information, write to publisher at address above.

For our children, with the fervent prayer that the Earth we leave them will be as liveable as the one we inherited.

ACKNOWLEDGMENTS

Halo Books wishes to acknowledge the people
behind the Evergreen Alliance.

Samm Coombs, Writer
Susan Larson, Concept and Design
Bob West, Associate Editor
Hal Larson, Editor & Publisher

Nancy May

Dick McLean

Christy Goodlett

Ralph Holmstad

Dick Rojas

Bob Sand

Faye Chang

Karen Mandel

Artype

Jane Smith

Jack DeCelle

Gretchen Hecht

Joan Checkley

Ecolokids

Park Rangers Jill and Less Allert
San Francisco Bay Area Regional Poison Center
Earthworks Paper Company

TABLE OF CONTENTS

I. **THE MEANING OF GREEN:** In recent years, the "Green" in Christmas has referred to the color of money. But that's changing: Nature's green is making a comeback. 🍃 It's easier on the eye as well as the pocketbook, 🍃 And it's much more in keeping with the spirit of Christmas.

II. **O' TANNENBAUM:** Come December 26th there will be 50 million fewer fir, spruce and pine trees in America. 🍃 All anyone ever wanted to know about selecting and caring for a living Christmas tree 🍃 And a little bit of history about the evergreen tradition.

III. **DECK THE HALLS:** All that glitters is not glitz! 🍃 Singing Trees. 🍃 Lids made lovely. 🍃 Ringstreamers 🍃 Origami Pinwheel 🍃 The Yule log. 🍃 Mistletoe is not for salads.

IV. **GIFTS THAT HELP:** A gallery of home-made green gifts 🍃 Help the helpful: good "green" causes. 🍃 "Green" stocking stuffers. 🍃 "Green" catalogs. 🍃 Growing gifts. 🍃 Water-saving gifts. 🍃 Gifts from the "green" library (young readers included). 🍃 Recycling gifts. Flea markets, Goodwill and Salvation Army stores. 🍃 Gifts to avoid.

V. **WRAPPING IT UP:** Why buy expensive foil and glossy papers that can't be recycled when something better is available in every home? 🍃 Paper alternatives. 🍃 Ties and Tags.

VI. **CELEBRATING ON THE JOB:** Christmas provides employers with hundreds of opportunities to help the environment. 🍃 Office parties and business gifts included. 🍃 Resolutions for a green working environment.

VII. **CHRISTMAS IN THE COMMUNITY:** How schools, clubs, and groups of all kinds can celebrate constructively 🍃 Being a green mentor.

VIII.   **CHRISTMAS TIME IS PARTY TIME:** How to celebrate today without denting tomorrow.  Christmas food  Drinks  Christmas shopping  The next day.

IX.   **BLESSED ARE THE CHILDREN:** If Christmas has never happened, kids would have invented it.  Children's party ideas.  First comes food.  Party favors  Kid's gifts  Games children play  Santa's wish list  Handle with care  It's their party.

X.   **CONSERVATION IN THE KITCHEN:** Tips on saving time, money and energy (yours and the guests') while preparing the festive feast.

XI.   **HAPPY NEW YEAR!** Making next year cleaner and greener.  Why little things mean a lot  Green resolutions.

GREEN IS ALWAYS
IN SEASON

When we published The First Green Christmas in 1990 (the first year of the Green Decade) a lot of experts warned about mixing ecological concerns with Christmas. "No one worries about the environment during the holidays," they claimed.

Well, as it turned out, enough of you were sufficiently concerned to make that little volume one of the season's Best Sellers!

That reception seemed to call for an encore — and a chance to include a lot of things overlooked the first time.

This second edition has been updated and expanded to include dozens of interesting ideas sent in by last year's readers. We also heard from many "Green" organizations and companies with environmentally sensitive products and services that deserve mention.

The Evergreen Alliance welcomed ideas that became helpful additions to the chapters on Gifts, Wrappings, Decorations, among others. This new edition features a whole new chapter for and about *Christmas with the children.* So there are even more reasons to read and enjoy this latest edition — and to give it to others.

Another lesson learned from that first edition has to do with timing. For maximum value, this book should be your *first* Christmas purchase. That will allow plenty of time to put some of the suggestions into practice. If you buy the book to give as a present, you might consider sending it as a kind of super Christmas Card. That way it will be opened the day it's received — in time to do some good.

We also should note that many of last year's readers suggested that the new edition provide help for other holidays as well. So we've tried to identify those ideas/products/practices that apply to any gift-giving time. Because *green is always in season.*

The Publisher

Hurt not the earth, neither the sea, nor the trees.
—Revelations 7:33

I.
THE MEANING
OF GREEN

Take a holiday from spending.

Once Upon A Time, before commerce hung a price tag around the neck of Christmas, the word "green" brought to mind Mother Nature's evergreenery.

Since the Industrial Revolution turned Christmas into a global merchandising event, *greenbacks* have replaced *evergreens*. This material turn has given us a holiday of a different hue. And while we all decry the commercialization of Jesus' birthday, is it really so terrible? After all, Christmas comes but once a year. How can such a brief lapse harm the planet?

The *real* price we pay for this annual consuming frenzy starts with the 50 million odd trees that are cut here in the U.S. — enough to cover all of Rhode Island with an evergreen blanket! And many times that number are felled to make wrapping paper and packaging materials. Our gutters runneth over with December's excess. The mountains of garbage that pile up the day after include tons of plastic and other non-recyclable refuse that will be with us for centuries.

All this celebrating consumes an incredible amount of non-renewable energy. This keeps our power plants working overtime, further degrading the environment and depleting our dwindling supply of fossil fuels.

It's a melancholy truth that some 70% of our discretionary purchases are made during November and December when we are least likely to be discriminating "green consumers."

As bad as this is, some environmentalists look in the other direction come the Christmas season, lest they be labelled Holiday killjoys. But the happy truth is you can have the merriest of Christmases while reducing the season's impact on the environment. And you can save plenty of greenbacks in the process.

With a little ingenuity and modest effort, anyone can have a Green Christmas. You can help make the world a better place simply by keeping the oven door closed, and using wrapping paper made from recycled paper.

That's one of the advantages of being a populous nation. When a few million people save a few watts, it adds up to millions of kilowatts, and thousands of barrels of foreign oil that don't have to be transported to our power plants.

Of course there's a lot more you can do to make this Christmas a truly green Christmas.

> *The care of the earth is our most ancient, most worthy and, after all, our most pleasing responsibility. To cherish what remains of it, and to foster its renewal, is our only legitimate hope.*
> — Wendall Berry

The Dear Old Tree

BY LUELLA WILSON SMITH

There's a dear old tree, an evergreen tree, And it blossoms once a year. 'Tis loaded with fruit from top to root, And it brings to all good cheer.

For it's blossoms bright are small candles white And it's fruit is dolls and toys. And they all are free for both you and me If we're good little girls & boys.

From *St. Nicholas* Magazine, Dec., 1907.

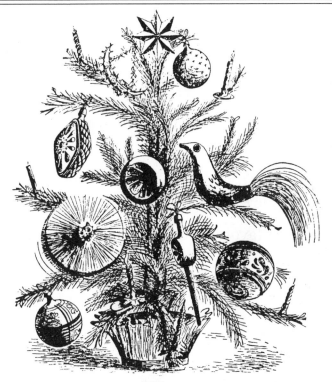

II.

O' TANNENBAUM

*The Evergreen Christmas tree is the heart
and herald of the holiday season.*

Whatever its size and genus — pine, spruce
or fir — the conical evergreen is the centerpiece
of Christmas. It fills homes with the fresh scent
of winterwoods and lights the way for Santa's
nocturnal visit. And come Christmas morning,
everyone gathers 'round the tree to open the
presents piled underneath.

Lore & Legend:
A SHORT HISTORY OF THE CHRISTMAS TREE.

Where did it all begin? There are probably as many legends as there are trees.

Our favorite is that Adam, when he packed up and left Paradise, took along an apple or sprout from the Tree of Knowledge. And from this came the tree from which the Cross was constructed.

Thus the first Christmas tree, if you buy the premise, was an apple tree.

Dissolve now to the Roman Empire. It is the January Kalends, and we see the Romans busily adorning their Trees of Life with decorations and candles, to commemorate the Saturnalia.

Fast-forward to medieval time. The idea of the Tree of Life has spread throughout Europe. But now the tree is decorated with apples and ribbons, as well as candles, celebrating the Light of the World.

Another sweet legend has Martin Luther

returning home after wandering one Christmas Eve under a winter sky sparkling with a million stars. He promptly set up a fir tree for his children and adorned it with countless candles — his homage to the glittering heaven that had so stirred him.

In fifteenth century England it was the Christmas custom to deck the house with holm, bays, ivy and whatever else was green and growing.

> *Never say there is nothing beautiful in the world any more. There is always something to make you wonder, in the shape of a tree, the trembling of a leaf.*
> —Albert Schweitzer

Because fir trees were not readily available in European cities or to those celebrants living in more southerly climes, a common substitute in the nineteenth century, and one still found in many country places around the globe, was the "pyramid", a construction adorned with colored paper, lights and in some cases, green twigs. This contrivance was kept from one Christmas to the next — the first re-usable Christmas decoration!

The first record of a Christmas tree on public display in the United States was in 1830.

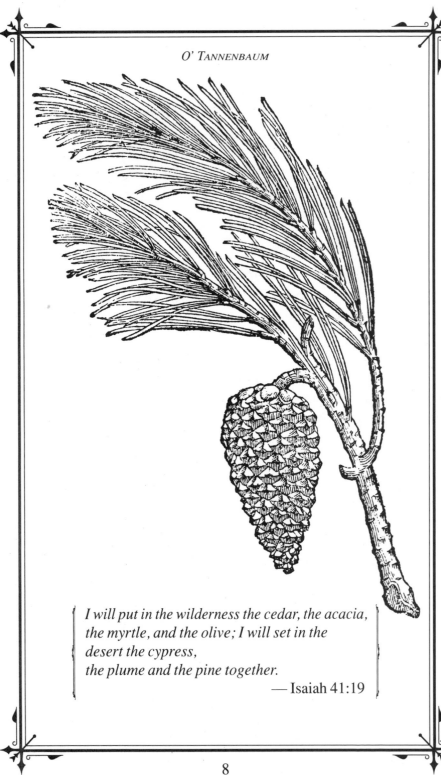

*I will put in the wilderness the cedar, the acacia,
the myrtle, and the olive; I will set in the
desert the cypress,
the plume and the pine together.*

— Isaiah 41:19

CUTTING DOWN ON CUTTING DOWN

In America's pioneer days, forests were abundant and trees were free for the chopping.

Today, however, we know every green growing thing is an asset to be protected. Some 50 million evergreens fall each year here in the U.S. in the name of Christmas, and an estimated 80 million worldwide are lost to the season.

> *Over increasing areas Spring now comes unheralded by the return of birds, and the early mornings are strangely silent where once they were filled with the beauty of bird song.*
> —Rachel Carson

It's true that more and more of the trees destined for harvesting are planted and grown for that purpose on "Christmas Tree Farms," minimizing the impact on our native forests. So don't feel guilty about cutting the family tree at one of those special-purpose tree farms.

However, you can make a positive contribution to the carbon dioxide cycle, reducing the so-called "greenhouse" gases in the atmosphere, by growing your own. And as long as you're at it, why not grow some more to give as presents two or three years hence.

There is something especially satisfying about fostering a tree — any tree, any time, anywhere. Parenting a Christmas tree that will be the center of attention during this sacred time of year is even more pleasurable.

You don't need a lot of land, or even a garden. A few pots and lots of TLC will do. A local nursery or garden supply store can tell you how.

Next best to growing your own is buying one already grown. A living Christmas tree is more expensive than a cut tree. But it doesn't take many Christmases before that living tree will start saving you money.

If your nurseryman sells it, you can assume the local climate/elevation/soil will sustain it. (A tree doesn't have to be a native of your locale to flourish there!)

There's also the matter of taste and decor to consider when choosing a living Christmas tree. Each species makes a different "statement." Consider color and texture; the kind of ornaments you will use — do they require space beneath the branches to hang gracefully, or is dense foliage okay?

Pines, for example, are usually the most dense and lend themselves to decorations that sit on or close to each bough. The texture of Scotch Pine is bold, informal. Whereas a Noble Fir's widely-spaced symmetry and short needles make for a more formal impression.

Durability isn't a consideration when selecting a living Christmas tree. But for the record, a cut fir lasts longest, all else being equal. Pines are next, with spruce the least durable.

> *My house is entirely enbosomed in high plane trees, with good grass below, and under them I breakfast, dine, write, read, and receive my company.*
>
> — Thomas Jefferson

THE TOP DOZEN

What is the ideal live Christmas tree?

Depends on where you live, what you want to spend, size requirements and how much growth you can accommodate in the future.

Also, consider whether you plan to plant it out or keep it in a container, and the kind of trees it will have for neighbors.

On the following pages is a chart of the dozen most popular species used for living Christmas trees.

DOUGLAS FIR	**NOBLE FIR**	**WHITE FIR**
(Pseudotsuga menziesii)	*(Abies procera)*	*(A. concolor)*
Nursery Sizes: 3 to 7 Feet	**Nursery Sizes** 3 to 6 feet	**Nursery Sizes** 1 to 6 feet
Price: $16 to $50	**Price:** $20 to $60	**Price:** $15 to $90
Container Growth: 1 to 2 Feet Yearly	**Container Growth:** 4 Inches Yearly	**Container Growth:** 1 to 4 Inches Yearly
Best Climates: North East and West, Midwest and Rockies	**Best Climates:** North East and West, Midwest and Rockies	**Best Climates:** Most Anywhere

NORWAY SPRUCE	DWARF ALBERTA SPRUCE	COLORADO BLUE SPRUCE
(Picea abies)	*(P. glauca 'conica')*	*(P. pungens 'Glauca')*
Nursery Sizes: 3 to 7 Feet	**Nursery Sizes** 1 to 4 feet	**Nursery Sizes** 1 to 6 feet
Price: $4 to $90	**Price:** $4 to $90	**Price:** $6 to $12
Container Growth: 2 to 12 Inches	**Container Growth:** 4 Inches Yearly in Youth Slows Later and Never Becomes Tall	**Container Growth:** 1 to 5 Inches Yearly
Best Climates: Most Anywhere Except: South and Deserts	**Best Climates:** Most Anywhere Except: Low and Intermediate Deserts	**Best Climates:** Most Anywhere

SCOTCH PINE	**NORFOLK ISLAND**	**JAPANESE BLACK PINE**
(Pinus sylvestris)	*(Araucaria heterophylla*	*(P. thubergiana)*
Nursery Sizes: 2 to 8 Feet	**Nursery Sizes** 1½ to 7 feet	**Nursery Sizes** 1½ to 6 feet
Price: $5 to $75	**Price:** $13 to $90	**Price:** $5 to $75
Container Growth: 1 to 2 Feet Yearly	**Container Growth: Indoors:** 7 inches Yearly **Outdoors:** 14 inches Yearly	**Container Growth:** 1½ to 2 Feet Yearly
Best Climates: North East and West, Midwest and Rockies	**Best Climates:** Tropical, Subtropical, Southwest, South Gulf Coast or as a Houseplant.	**Best Climates:** Most Anywhere

ALEPPO PINE	**MONTEREY PINE**	**MONDELL PINE**
(*P. halepensis*) *menziesii*	(*P. radiata*)	(*P. eldarica*))
Nursery Sizes: 2 to 6 Feet	**Nursery Sizes** 2 to 8 feet	**Nursery Sizes** 1 to 8 feet
Price: $4 to $65	**Price:** $12 to $75	**Price:** $6 to $70
Container Growth: Fast—2 to 6 Feet Yearly	**Container Growth:** Fast—2 to 8 Feet Yearly	**Container Growth:** Fast—1 to 8 Feet Yearly
Best Climates: South, Southwest and Low and Intermediate Deserts	**Best Climates:** North, Midwest, East, West in Low Elevations	**Best Climates:** Southwest

Tree Care and Feeding

Don't plan to keep a living tree indoors more than two weeks, three weeks maximum. And don't position it close to any heat sources, including an unshaded south-facing window. Set it in water after spraying with an antitranspirant to help prevent moisture loss.

Heat-generating Christmas tree lights do minimal damage when they come in contact with the needles, and this can be minimized with the new "cool" 5W lights being sold this year.

Your living tree arrives in a peat pot or metal can, neither of which is particularly Christmassy. There are a number of can wraps that provide a festive facade while adding to the tree's dignity.

These trees in pots can get heavy. One easy way to move them is on your kid's skateboard.

Give your tree a good soaking before bringing it in. Best to do this a day or two early, so it doesn't create a puddle on the floor.

You should water your tree every three days it is in the house. Idea is to keep the soil moist.

To give your tree time-released watering try using ice cubes. The tree continues to get water as the cubes melt.

> *A living tree will never become a torch.*
> —Andrew Casper

YOUR LIVING TREE LIVES ON

The real beauty of a living Christmas tree is that it stays around all year to provide photosynthesis, shade, aroma and beauty. It gives you "Christmas every day."

Think carefully about where you want the tree to live until next Christmas: in its container or in the ground. Consult your nursery for advice about your specific tree.

Generally, if it was taken from the ground this Christmas, you should keep it out of high wind locations and give it part shade.

Fertilize in Spring and Summers. Fish emulsion is a good fertilizer, and slow-release chemicals are also recommended.

After two or three years, your tree may become cramped in its pot. Because you don't want it to outgrow your house, you'll need to artfully prune its roots — a subject too detailed for this forum. There are guides to this gentle art at any nursery or library.

RECYCLING CUT TREES

When it comes time to dispose of your cut tree, one option is to take it to a local nursery that has facilities for composting trees. Or, if you have your own compost pile, cut the branches into small pieces; the trunk can be saved for firewood. If it's a pine tree, save the needles; they make great mulch for your garden.

Although burning those dry branches and brittle needles in the fireplace creates a roaring fire, however brief, it's not good practice because of the pine tar it distributes in your flu and chimney. Play it safe and recycle the needles and branches as suggested.

What To Do With Non-Living Trees

Artificial trees made from plastic and metal pose a different problem. They can't be recycled, and we want to keep them out of our refuse stream. In fact, the whole idea of artificial trees is to keep them for reuse. And when you don't want yours any longer, donate it to someone else; young folks starting out; a home for the elderly; a hospice; orphanage. Your dead tree still has a life for someone.

Your Very Own Memorial Christmas Tree Grove

Some families with large lots buy a new living Christmas tree each season. In time, they will have a small forest of trees from Christmases past — a nice way to create a monument to each Christmas.

Living Christmas trees also make the ideal green Christmas gift. Those that are small enough to mail become someone's personal tree, and in time, will grow into a family tree!

Now, some ideas for decorating your living Christmas tree, and the use of other forms of evergreenery.

III.
DECK THE HALLS

*The new fashion in Christmas
decorations is old-fashioned.*

The way we celebrate Christmas says a lot
about our past as well as our future. This new
Christmas of the "green decade" is an opportunity to demonstrate our new environmental
awareness. And what better way than by our
choice of decorations. These ornamental sym-
bols set the mood and define the attitude of
your household.

EDIBLE ORNAMENTS

If "natural," "homemade," "old-fashioned" and "traditional" describe the feeling you want your decorations to convey, a good place to start is with **popcorn** or **cranberry strings**. Drape these around the tree instead of phony flocking or metallic "icicles."

Popcorn and **cranberries** can also be shaped into ornamental stars and hearts by stringing them on medium gauge wire, bent to the desired shape. Add a bow and hang them from your tree and other appropriate places.

Sweet **candy wreaths** are also easy to make, but be careful to pick a candy that can be strung, and won't go soft and drip chocolate on the carpet.

The best thing about **cookie ornaments** is how easily they disappear after Christmas; no packing necessary. Use a dough that's sturdy: gingerbread or sugar cookie dough. Poke a hole at the tip using a drinking straw. Thread a ribbon through it, tie in a large loop and hang on a bough of your tree.

ORGANIC DECORATIONS

Your garden is probably full of good ideas for Christmas ornaments. **Rosettes** of pine cones, fallen branches and clumps of berries artfully done up with a beautiful bow are great for the mantlepiece. Include a few red apples, and you have the perfect centerpiece for your Christmas feast.

Clusters of pine cones, red berries and evergreen sprigs at each place-setting echo the centerpiece, but take care: Holly berries are poisonous and should be avoided near food.

Wreathed Greenery

Wreaths, like Christmas trees, are a part of the ancient tradition of bringing evergreens indoors around the time of the winter solstice as a symbol of life everlasting. In pre-Christian times the peoples of Egypt, the Mideast, the Orient, and Europe made wreaths from evergreens as well as herbs and other materials.

For your family's Christmas wreath, use an evergreen linked by custom and legend to Christmas: fir, rosemary, holly, ivy and/or mistletoe.

Also popular for wreath-making are spruce, hemlock, balsam, fir, yew and pine branches, as well as bay and laurel leaves.

Or make an untraditional wreath by weaving corn husks looped through wire.

As an alternative to the classic wreath, make a festive door-hanging by fashioning a swag of waxy, leathery leaves that are naturally durable — e.g., aucuba, boxwood, madrone, Oregon grape, toyon or Southern magnolia — integrated with mossy twigs, citrus and seed pods. Chili peppers braided with strings of garlic are a popular choice, particularly in their native Southwest.

Magical, Mystical Mistletoe

According to ancient custom, this parasitical evergreen has many magical properties that are most powerful at Christmastime.

Mistletoe was considered sacred in pre-Christian Europe. The Druid priests used it in sacrifices. The Celts believed it had miraculous healing powers. It was variously credited with curing diseases, rendering poisons harmless, making humans and animals fertile, and protecting the house from ghosts.

In eighteenth-century England, mistletoe was credited with a different kind of magic. If a couple kissed beneath it, romance could not be far away. Like so many Old Wives Tales, this one has as many sources as there are Old Wives. According to Norse myth, one of God's arrows made of mistletoe struck down Balder, son of Frigga. Crying tears of white berries, she brought her son back to life and vowed to kiss anyone who rested beneath the plant.

Quite a different version explains mistletoe's adoption as a Christmas ritual. Under its influence "a Holy kiss of pardon and redemption" was initiated by the priest and passed through the congregation. A nice custom any time of year.

> *The damsel donned her kirtle sheen; the hall was dressed with holly green; forth to the wood did merry men go, to gather in the mistletoe.*
>
> —Sir Walter Scott

AROMATIC ORNAMENTS

Hang a **pomander ball** dotted with patches of orange rind and cloves for a holiday scent. Or cover a small cardboard ring in glue and dip into a bin of **potpourri**. **Rosemary** sprigs can be fashioned into a fragrant decorative tree that sits on a wreath made of cinnamon sticks. Fashion a heart-shaped lace sachet filled with **lavender.**

Perhaps the loveliest scent of the holiday is the evanescent aroma of baking that wafts through the house before Christmas. By the time guests arrive, alas, the kitchen has been cleaned and those wonderful smells never reach visitors' noses.

There are, however, other ways to add nose-tingling scents. Throw cinnamon sticks, whole allspice, a lemon, an orange, and apple peelings into a saucepan full of water. Bring it to boil, then simmer.

A fire of cedar or pine will transport you to the North Woods. Juniper incense or chips will add to the pleasure.

Or place a drop of your favorite perfume onto a light bulb. The hot air generated by the lit bulb will fill the room with a special allure.

A SINGING TREE

Theme trees are all the rage, and what theme is more joyous and universal than Christmas music? Make novel decorations with sheet music of your favorite carols, making 8 x 10 or smaller Xerox copies for hanging with a toy musical instrument, a sprig of holly secured by red ribbon. Or roll up the sheet music (not too tightly), wrap with red ribbon and hang. When it comes time to sing, no one will be at a loss for words!

ORIGAMI PINWHEEL

This is a little complicated for origami first-timers, but worth the effort.

Begin with a square piece of remnant wrapping, computer, bond or colored paper.

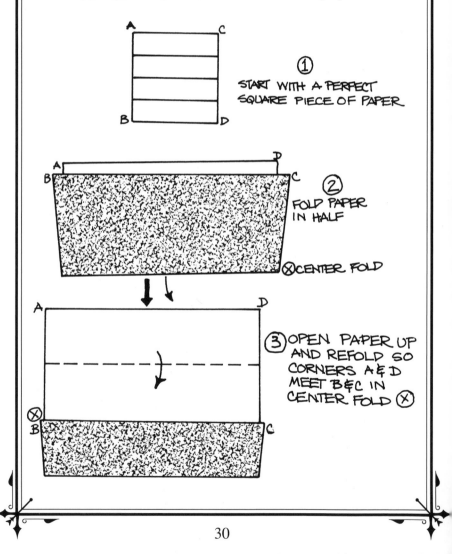

① START WITH A PERFECT SQUARE PIECE OF PAPER

② FOLD PAPER IN HALF

⊗ CENTER FOLD

③ OPEN PAPER UP AND REFOLD SO CORNERS A & D MEET B & C IN CENTER FOLD ⊗

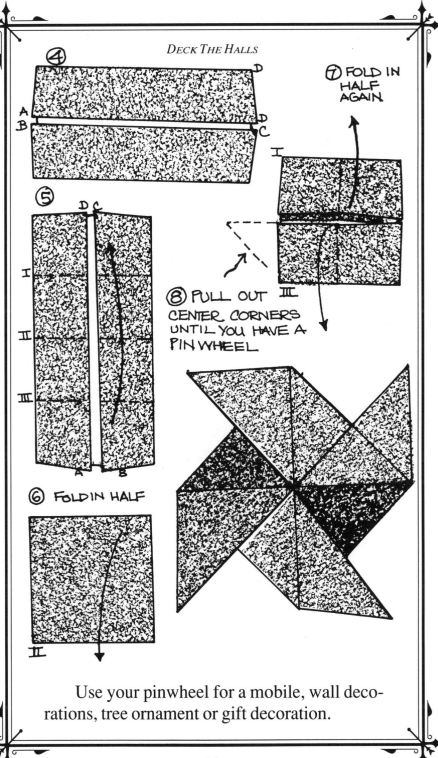

④

⑤

⑥ FOLD IN HALF

⑦ FOLD IN HALF AGAIN

⑧ PULL OUT CENTER CORNERS UNTIL YOU HAVE A PINWHEEL

Use your pinwheel for a mobile, wall decorations, tree ornament or gift decoration.

LIDS MADE LOVELY

Here's an inventive way to recycle old plastic lids.

Cut out interesting small pictures from old magazines or Christmas cards. Glue one or more on the lid. Add old beads, buttons, or jewelry for sparkle. Punch a hole, pull string or yarn through it, and you have a handsome hanging decoration.

RINGSTREAMERS

Make a festive outdoor Ringstreamer out of fabric, string and a plastic lid. It's simple, seasonal and stylish.

You create a ring by cutting away the middle of a plastic lid. Now get a few of dad's old or unwanted ties — or cut two-inch strips of colorful fabric about the length of a tie.

Knot three ties or fabric strips around the ring, creating two streamers of equal length from each.

Now tie a string around the opposite side of the ring and hang it to wave in the breeze.

LET THERE BE LIGHT

One illuminating idea is to collect a bunch of tin cans; fill them full of water and freeze. Now it will be easy to punch holes in the shape of fir trees or stars around the sides. Use big nails if you don't have a proper punch. For a top, buy aluminum funnels with a necklace of holes punched in it. Place a votive candle at the bottom.

The idea is not to make better decorations, but to create *your* decorations. In the process, you'll save a pile of greenbacks and a few trips to the store.

WINDOW PAINTINGS

What child can resist the opportunity to cover the windows with giant cutouts of Christmas graffiti. A fir tree, Santa, reindeer and stars are favorite subjects.

THE YULE LOG

Most logs are for burning, but not this one — not yet. In many a household, it's part of the Christmas tradition to select and decorate a log that sits in the fireplace as a centerpiece. In addition to the usual bright red bow, secure pine cones in drilled holes.

What, Father Christmas here again? With Yule Log on your back and mighty store of racy things well stuffed within your pack.
— Christmas verse, 1848

IV.
GIFTS THAT HELP

*Everything we give to
the earth we get back.*

The best Christmas gifts are the "green"
kind: those that help revitalize our planet. And
high on this list must surely be The Tree. What
else grows into a monument and does so much
good every inch of the way?

Trees breathe life into our planet. They cool our cities; prevent erosion; reduce energy needs. Trees are the best defense against a warming climate. By absorbing CO_2, they combat the greenhouse effect. One tree eliminates hundreds of pounds of carbon dioxide every year. It takes a whole acre of trees to offset the emissions produced by a single automobile traveling 26,000 miles.

For long-distance giving, there are easy-to-mail starter kits for growing trees from seed. Pot, soil, seed and instructions all are included. It's like giving birth to one of nature's noblest creations. For personal delivery, select some inexpensive seedlings from your nurseryman, who will help you select a species to suit the specific situation: indoors or outdoors: for planting in a pot or the ground.

EXTEND CHRISTMAS INTO SPRING

Of course Mother Nature welcomes any kind of green growing thing, including a hillside blanketed with wildflowers. A packet of seeds costs very little and promises a big surprise come Spring. Most nurseries offer local favorites. You can also order by mail from wildflower specialists:

Moon Mountain Wildflowers, Box 34, Morro Bay, CA 93442.

Native Plants Inc., Box 177, Lehi, Utah 84043.

Larner Seeds, Box 407, Bolinas, CA 94924.

Wildflower Seed Co., Box 406, St. Helena, CA 94574.

Southwestern Native Seeds, Box 5053, Tucson, AZ 85703.

Also in the flora category of gift, consider this easy-to-make **Gift terrarium**.

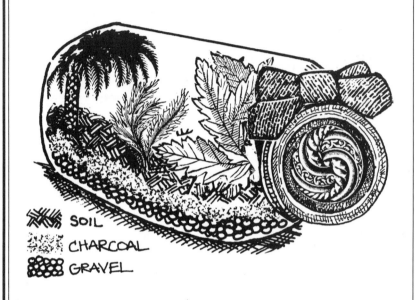

SOIL
CHARCOAL
GRAVEL

Select any wide-mouth, attractively-shaped clear jar (a ½-gallon juice jar is fine) with a lid. Add 1 to 2 inches (depending on jar's size) of pea gravel, about an inch of charcoal, and 1 to 2 inches of potting soil. Set down inside one or more houseplants. Ferns are an ideal choice. Add more potting soil to the top of the root ball. Lightly moisten soil and close lid. Display it in a well-lighted area out of direct sunlight. More water is usually not needed; the terrarium transpires, creating its own moisture.

A verdant variation is this bright **Berry Bowl**.

Into a rose bowl like this, put green moss, root and soil side up, in the bottom. Arrange small greens (like partridge berry or checkerberry) around the inside of the bowl.

Press the roots down softly. The bowl should be about half full. Sprinkle with water. Cover tightly with a clear plastic wrap and tie with a ribbon.

SPEAKING OF MOISTURE...

When giving plants, try to select those identified as "natives" or "drought-resistant," whether or not your locale is suffering a water-shortage. There's a new breed of nursery cropping up across the country specializing in these plants. Your local water district may well offer a list of those requiring little or no water once established. Not only will these plants save precious water; "natives" won't suffer from unusually hot or cold weather, else they would never have become indigenous.

BEYOND THE POINSETTIA

Christmas plants make a great calling card or office gift. But don't always select the ubiquitous poinsettia; there are many other colorful plants that go with Christmas. Among them: Kalanchoe, Freesia, Narcissus, Cyclamen, Chrysanthemum, Miniature Roses and Christmas cactus.

GIVE A GARDEN

It's a thoughtful and easy-to-do holiday gift. Simply assemble all the elements needed for a garden project. A salad garden, for example, would include gloves, lettuce plants or seeds, planting mix, and a shallow pot. For a rose garden, include a deep pot, soil, pruning shears and dry root roses. An herb garden is another thoughtful gift.

Any gift of plants, flowers or trees can make good use of old plastic bottles (quart, half-gallon or gallon sizes) by cutting off the upper portion and scalloping the top edge. To decorate, tie a green ribbon around the base and/or use decals or felt-tip markers.

WATER-CONSERVING GIFTS

In the earth's more populous areas, water fit for drinking is in short supply. And with intermittent droughts coupled with unrelenting population increases, shortages will become chronic in the 90s.

Here are some gifts that will abate waste and make a gallon do what used to take three, four or five gallons!

A nozzle with a shut-off valve will save hundreds of gallons in the hands of a car-washer.

A low-flow showerhead will save 3 to 5 gallons a minute per shower, and the bather will never know the difference.

Screw-on low-flow aerators for bath and kitchen faucets will reduce water use by 50%, or an average of 300 gallons per month for a family of four.

Instead of blade shaving, usually accomplished with a hot water running, switch to *a wind-up shaver* — no electricity needed; no water required: you'll save up to 20 gallons per shave.

For more on this subject, $3 buys you The Rocky Mountain Institute's "Water Efficiency For Your Home," a pamphlet you can obtain through the Seventh Generation catalog. For a broader view, send $9 to the National Water Center, P.O. Box 264, Eureka Springs, AR 72632, for their definitive guide to water conservation, *"We All Live Downstream".*

Give Something Of Yourself

The following do-it-yourself gift ideas cost little or nothing and are easily and quickly accomplished without a lot of tools and talent.

Flea-Free Fido: If you have a dog and live near any eucalyptus trees, gather the bell-shaped pods you'll find lying around underneath. With a heavy-duty needle threaded with dental floss, string them through the soft centers and slip the necklace around the dog's neck. People like the nice tangy smell, but fleas can't stand it!

Edible Christmas Cards: Bake a greeting card to show you care. Make a giant version of your favorite cookie, put a personal greeting on with icing, and watch your friends eat it up.

A Gift For The Birds: Spread sugarless peanut butter on pine cones. Like kids, birds love peanut butter, and it provides protein and oils for healthy feathers and bodies. Fasten the cones to the branches of a tree using floral wire.

PEANUT BUTTER

SEEDS

Another gift for our fine-feathered friends is a simple bird-feeder made from a half-gallon milk carton. Cut a "window" from the side of the carton and place a dowel or small tree branch from side-to-side beneath the window with the ends poking through holes on either side. Fill the bottom with bird seed and hang from the top, using a sturdy waxed line like fishing line or cat gut leader material.

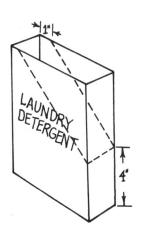

Soapbox Magazine Holder: Save all those giant-size (49-oz.) laundry detergent boxes. With an X-acto knife or scissors, cut from the top down each side at an angle to a point approximately 4" from the bottom. If the person it's intended for saves National Geographic Magazines, glue a photo collage of exotic, faraway places on the outside. If the holder is intended for the readers of a weekly news magazine, cut out "1992" and combine with current affairs pictures. If the subject is business, choose business-like pictures. It's a thoughtful gift and a practical way to put old cardboard to good use.

NEW GIFTS FROM OLD JUNK

Recycle old jewelry, ribbons, foil, buttons, beads, fabric — into attractive new gifts.

Start by visiting your five and dime, flea market, old jewelry drawer and sewing box for the necessaries: throw-away stuff you can convert into a host of different gift items.

Now string unlikely pieces into a unique necklace. Or glue a pin onto them for a decorative stickpin. Or mount them on a ribbon for a handsome hanging decoration. Or arrange them in a pattern on cloth and frame it for a different kind of collage. Or put them on earring clips.

Your gift is pretty, personal and original.

GLUE OLD BUTTONS ON CARDBOARD STRIP, ATTACH A CLASP AND YOU HAVE A BROACH.

CREATIVE COMMEMORATIVE GIFT

You can help friends celebrate a special event in their life by using the previous technique with items related to the event.

Gather photos, toys, memorabilia, invitations, announcements, awards, etc.

If they're flat, put 'em in a memory book or collage. If they're three-dimensional, help your friends remember with a special shadow box.

Don't forget **hot mitts, pot holders, knitted stocking caps, teapot cozies, log carriers, tote bags, aprons, finger puppets** and a **backscratcher** made from throwaway wire coat hangers (also good for plant hangers).

GIVE WARMTH

On a long winter's night, there's nothing like a roaring fire. But before a fire can roar, it must be started. So consider a gift of **firestarters** made from pine cones. They take a little effort, but make a thoughtful gift. Melt a bunch of candle stubs (colored preferred) or old crayon bits in the top of a double broiler. Remove and save the wicks. Quickly dip cones in the hot wax and lay on their side on a piece of

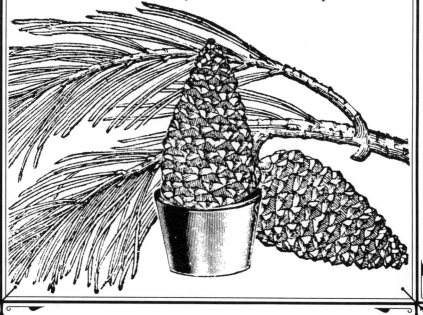

waxed paper. Now half-fill muffin tins with hot wax, place wicks on the edge of each and lower wax-coated cones into each basin. Allow to cool. To remove, place muffin tin in freezer for 5 or 10 minutes. Turn it upside down and cones will fall out. Place under wood and light. As the cone burns, pitch and wax collect on the wood above, making it ignite quickly. To package, place in a basket or cookie tin.

A major gift for someone special is a **goosedown comforter**. It'll save a modest fortune in heating bills and contribute to a good night's sleep every night.

On a budget? A good old-fashioned **hot-water bottle** or **warm wooly pajamas** are always appreciated.

How about an **automatic thermostat** that turns the heat down at night, up in the morning.

GIFTS FROM THE SUN

Some solar-powered gifts to brighten lives and save energy:

Solar battery chargers and rechargeable batteries. **Sunwatt Corporation**, P.O. Box 751, Addison, ME 04606. Phone 207/497-2204.

A **solar garden lamp** for patios and walkways. Provides five hours of night light. **Chronar Sunenergy**, P.O. Box 177, Princeton, NJ 08542. Phone 207/497-2204.

A **solar-powered radio and earphones**. Gives you four hours of play for each three hours in the sun. **Solar Electric Engineering**, 175 Cascade Court, Rohnert Park, CA 94928. Phone 707/586-1987.

A **4-in-1 Solar Construction Kit** for youngsters to make solar-powered airplanes, helicopters and windmills. Also a safari hat, tea jar, flashlight — even a solar-powered speedboat. **Jade Mountain**, P.O. Box 4616, Boulder, CO 80306. Phone 303/449-6601.

Sun Prints demonstrate the artistic side of solar energy. When the light-sensitive paper is exposed to the sun, a positive image appears where objects have touched the paper. Image changes to negative when developed in tap water.

RECYCLED GIFTS

One child's discard is another's delight. **Flea Markets** are stuffed with perfectly good toys at next-to-nothing prices. Same goes for **Salvation Army & Goodwill** Industries stores (where the old stuff has been made new again).

GIFTS FROM THE "GREEN LIBRARY":

It's A Matter Of Survival, by Suzuki and Gordon (*Harvard University Press*, 278 pages, $19.95), the same folks who bring you the acclaimed radio show of the same name. In this new book, the authors make clear that we either revolutionize the human agenda in the 1990s or watch the world become uninhabitable by 2040.

Everything you ever wanted to know about waste will be found in **Wasting Away**, (*Sierra Club Books*, 270 pages; $30), by Kevin Leach and Michael Southworth.

The best way to reduce waste, of course, is

to recycle — a subject about which everyone has questions. All the answers will be found in the Earthworks new book, **The Recycler's Handbook**.

The TreePeople, a Los Angeles-based non-profit organization that has helped plant millions of trees in urban areas is extending their outreach with a new book, **The Simple Act Of Planting A Tree**, written by Andy and Katie Lipkis (*Jeremy P. Tarcher*, Inc., 236 pages, $12.95).

Home & Family Guide: Practical Action for the Environment, available through *The Harmony Foundation of Canada* PO 4016, Station C, Ottowa, Ontario K1Y 4P12. For orders outside Canada, send $8.50 including postage and handling.

Trashing the Planet: How Science Can Help Us Deal With Acid Rain, Depletion of the Ozone, and the Soviet Threat (Among Other Things), by Dixy Lee Ray and Louis Guzzo (*Regnery Gateway*).

The Kid's Nature Book, *Williamson Publishing*, provides a day-by-day guide, listing 365 things kids can do for their planet.

HELP THE HELPFUL

Here's a list of worthwhile non-profit organizations which are always strapped for the means to do good. And your gift is tax deductible. These groups will send a nice acknowledgement to whomever you name.

The Audubon Society is at the forefront of every fight to save birds' habitat. National Audubon Society, 645 Pennsylvania Ave., SE, Washington, D.C. 20003.

Earth Island Institute, 300 Broadway, Ste. 28, San Francisco, CA 94133; 415/788-3666, Supports international projects protecting and restoring the environment. A $25 membership includes the quarterly Earth Island Journal.

Environmental Defense Fund, 257 Park Ave. S, New York, NY 10010; 212/505-2100, is concerned with water pollution, pesticides, wildlife preservation, wetlands protection, rain forests, toxic rain, the ozone layer, toxic chemicals and waste. The $20 annual membership includes the quarterly *EDF Newsletter.*

Friends of the Earth, 530 7th St. SE, Washington, DC 20003; 202/544-2600, promotes the conservation, protection and rational use of the earth and its land-based and oceanic resources. Memberships run $25 ($15 for students, senior citizens), and include the monthly magazine, *No Man Apart.*

Friends of the Urban Forest is dedicated to the proposition that cities need trees, too. 116 New Montgomery,# 526, San Francisco, CA 94105. (415) 541-9144.

Greenpeace, 1436 U St. NW, Washington, DC 20009; 202/462-1177, has concentrated its efforts on halting the wanton killing of marine mammals and other endangered creatures, toxic waste reduction and nuclear disarmament. The $20 annual membership provides the bimonthly Greenpeace magazine.

Greenhouse Crisis Foundation, 1130 17th St. NW, Ste 630, Washington, DC 20036; 202/466-2823, is dedicated to creating a global awareness of the greenhouse crisis.

Our Earth, Ourselves: The Action-Oriented Guide to Help You Protect and Preserve Our Environment by Ruth Caplan (Bantam).

Home Safe Home: How to Make Your Home Environmentally Safe, by William Kelly (Acropolis Press).

Earth Right: Every Citizen's Guide, by Patricia Hynes (Prima Publishing).

Clearer, Cleaner, Safer, Greener: A Blueprint for Detoxifying Your Environment by Gary Null (Villard Books).

Teenage Survival Manual, by Samm Coombs (Discovery Books), $9.95.

The Planet of Trash, An Environmental Fable, by George Poppel (National Press), $9.95.

The Nature Conservancy, 1815 N. Lynn St., Arlington, VA 22209; 703/841-5300, acts to preserve ecosystems and the rare species they shelter. The $15 annual membership gives you a bimonthly magazine, *The Nature Conservancy Magazine*.

Rainforest Action Network, 430 E. University, Ann Arbor, MI 48109; 313/764-2147, focuses on the preservation, protection and rational use of rain forests. $10 donation includes its newsletter, *Tropical Echoes*, published every six weeks.

Sierra Club, 730 Polk St., San Francisco, CA 94109; 415/776-2211, promotes conservation of the natural environment. Make a gift of a $33 membership (includes subscription to the monthly magazine *Sierra*, which is worth the price of admission).

The Wilderness Society, 900 Seventeenth St., NW, Washington, DC 20005;202/842-3400, protects wildlands, wildlife, forests, parks, rivers and shorelines. First year membership is $15. Includes a quarterly magazine, *The Wilderness*.

World Wildlife Fund, 416/923-8173, saves our dwindling rainforests. For $25 you can save an acre. Use Mastercard, Visa, check or money order. You'll receive a packet with decal and certificate identifying the recipient as a Guardian of the Amazon.

GREEN STOCKING STUFFERS

There are a host of new environmental magazines, most of which are slick, glossy showcases (albeit printed on recycled paper). Among the most impressive and informative:

Buzzworm, a bimonthly ecology journal that rates a place on any coffee table. (1818 16th Street, Boulder, CO 80302.)

E The Environmental Magazine is another beauty, And why not; the purview is Nature, in all its many-splendored glory. (P.O. Box 5098, Westport, CT 06881.)

Garbage Journal is full of practical tips for ecological action at home. (435 Ninth St., Brooklyn, NY 11215.)

The **New Environmentalist** is the handiwork of a former senior editor at *Time*, Russ Hoyle, who has filled the monthly columns with in-depth coverage to provide readers with answers to their immediate and practical concerns about the environment. (460 Park Ave., New York, NY 10002.)

And don't forget the old standbys, *Sunset* and *National Geographic*.

Other stocking-sized gifts include **tickets to a local nature museum** and a **pocket-sized field guide** that identifies flora and fauna. Also, **bicycling and hiking path maps** may be found in local book stores. And your local health food stores are well-stocked with **biodegradable soaps and shampoos**.

GIFTS FROM GREEN CATALOGS

The Green movement has spawned a raft of environmentally-sensitive catalogs — i.e., catalogs offering know-how and merchandise that help the environment. Ordering by mail eliminates shopping trips, which reduces air pollution, ozone depletion and the emission of greenhouse gases. And stamps are still cheaper than gasoline.

Smith & Hawken puts out an excellent catalog to help the organic gardener. 125 Corte Madera, Mill Valley, CA 94941. Or call (415) 38-2000.

One of the most noteworthy new catalogs is one produced just for kids. It's called **Ecol-O-Kids** and what a joy it is. Especially the graphics. Write for a copy at 3146 Shadow Lane, Topeka, KS 66604. Better yet, call 913/232-4747. It's packed with positive presents, including calendars, videos, books, stationery sets, green apparel.

The Sound of Music: *A Gentle Wind* (Box 3103, Albany, NY 12203) will send you a catalog full of recorded music for children with themes of sharing and caring for each other and the planet.

The Seventh Generation (Products For A Healthy Earth) is a case study on how to do well doing good. The title derives from the Great Law of the *Hau de no saunee*, "In our every deliberation, we must consider the impact of our decisions on the next seven generations." They ask $2 for their catalog, called an "Environmental Product Guide," and it's well worth it. There is also an Environmental Book Catalog that's free. For both, write Seventh Generation, Colchester, VT 05446-1672.

One of the more innovative Green catalogs is one called **Co-op America Catalog** ("A Marketplace For Peace, Cooperation and a Healthy Planet"). Co-op America is a membership organization that links socially responsible businesses with consumers interested in purchasing socially responsible goods and services. They not only test every product (in order to guarantee it); they put the provider of that product or service to an equally rigid test. Each of two catalogs issued every year offers over 300 products from more than 100 "Green" businesses — everything from canvas shopping bags to Rainforest Crunch (candy). To get on their catalog mailing list, write Co-op America Catalog, 2100 M Street, Ste 403, P.O. 18217, Washington, DC 20036. Or call (202) 223-1881.

Besides "general merchandise" catalogs, there are specialty catalogs featuring organic food products:

Gracious Living Organic Farms, General Delivery, Insko, KY 41443, specializes in mail order fruits and veggies (of the organic kind).

Cherry Hill Cannery, Inc., Barre-Montpelier Rd, MR 1, Barrew, VT 05641 (802/479-2558) is a worker-owned cooperative making natural and organic foods: maple syrup, apple butter, assorted fruit sauces — over 120 yummy items. Ask for free catalog.

Mad River Farm, P.O. 155, Arcata, CA 95521 (707/822-7150) has a catalog full of handmade jams and marmalades, including kiwi jam, rasp-rhubarb jam, and lemon marmalade ... all made from organic fruit.

Mountain Springs, 356 W. Redview Dr., Monroe, UT 84754 (207/542-2303) deals in canned rainbow trout fillets from fish raised in pollutant-free springs.

Martha's Lemon Curd, P.O. Box 483, Lagunitas, CA 94938 (415/488-0323) makes this traditional all-natural, no-preservatives Scottish spread (the English call it Lemon Butter) so good you'll want to spoon it from jar to lips without waiting for the muffins to toast. Also, lemon topping for waffles, cakes and ice cream.

Many of the Green organizations listed under "Help The Helpful" offer catalogs packed with great Green gifts, including **The World Wildlife Fund, Sierra Club, National Wildlife Federation, Rainforest Action Network, The Nature Conservancy, National Audubon Society, The Cousteau Society and Greenpeace**.

GIVE A NATURE WALK

Here's a do-it-yourself gift you don't have to buy or make: a hike on the wild side! The giver leads the way to some special place you want to share with one or more friends, relatives and neighbors.

If you don't live near the woods or shore, plan an urban trek. Any city park is full of sights and sounds that are ordinarily overlooked.

Gifts To Avoid

Some gift items should be avoided — not because they pose a danger, but because they are endangered:

Furs: Seals and other marine mammals as well as polar bear, jaguar, tiger, snow leopard, ocelot, margay: a few endangered friends.

Ivory: Only Elephants wear ivory. Avoid scrimshaw, carvings, sculpture, boxes, jewelry — ivory in any form.

Exotic plants: certain cycads, orchids and cacti face extinction due to wholesale removal from their native habitat.

Exotic birds, animals, reptiles: If they aren't found in your area, they are better left where they belong.

Tropical hardwoods in the form of little boxes, bowls or carvings are fast depleting earth's forests of mahogany, teak, rosewood and satinwood.

Also to be avoided are **throwaways**: single-use items like razors, pens, cameras, clothing. The planet is already choking on our garbage without adding more such junk to our landfills. Anything **plastic** should be considered unfriendly to the environment, especially those things that are likely to be trashed in short order — e.g., toys, trinkets, keyholders, gimcracks and other novelties. **Electrical gizmos** of all sorts require power that could be used for more worthy purposes.

V.
WRAPPING IT UP

There are wiser ways to wrap gifts –
ways that don't add to the Christmas clutter.

It's anyone's guess how many trees are sacrificed each year to make paper for Christmas gift wrapping.

RECYCLED PAPER

One way to reduce this waste is to purchase Christmas cards and wrapping material made from recycled paper. That won't cost the earth another tree, and this material can be recycled again. This year, there should be a large selection of recycled giftwrap on the market. If you can't find any in your area, you can order by mail.

One of the many paper product companies specializing in gift wrap and greeting cards made from recycled paper is **Brush Dance**, 218 Cleveland Court, Mill Valley, CA 94941 (415) 389-6228. They offer a free catalog that includes notecards and stationery. Another is **Earth Care Paper Company**. No line of recycled paper products is more attractive than theirs. Wrapping papers and greeting cards feature original art that's really original! They also produce a marvelous array of paper for all seasons and reasons, including stationery and office supplies. For a free copy of their retail or wholesale papers (specify which), write them at P.O. Box 14140, Madison, Wisconsin 53714-0140 or call (608) 277-2920.

You can always fill your gift list with presents that require no wrapping. (In the previous chapter, we mentioned a number of possibilities — such as giving to good causes that send an acknowledgement of your gift to the recipient on recycled paper.)

Recycled Wrappings

Yet another way to wrap your gifts without adding to the earth's disposal dilemma is to create colorful wrappings from material you already have lying around.

This offers the additional benefit of putting something of yourself into the wrap. It's creative, fun, and ecologically smart.

Some easy-to-do suggestions:

❖ Paste old Christmas cards on old shopping bags.

❖ Use old maps or posters.

❖ Wrap your gifts to children in old colored comic pages.

❖ Personalize the wrapping by using selected magazine pages.

❖ Decorate brown paper grocery bags with a rubber stamp of your favorite Christmas design, using red and green ink pads, or use crayons and water colors.

❖ Beautify old butcher or kraft paper with homemade stamps fashioned from kitchen sponges cut into the shape of a Christmas tree, star, or other holiday symbol — or use half slices of citrus fruit dipped in acrylic paint.

❖ Use leftover wallpaper or wallpaper sample books

❖ Reuse wrappings from gifts you receive.

❖ Wrap with the pages of large old calendars

❖ Recycle tissue paper from prior purchases.

❖ Color yesterday's front page.

❖ Paste old playing cards to box.

❖ Wrap with old sheet music.

❖ Use kids' drawings or coloring book pages.

PAPER ALTERNATIVES

There's no rule that says gifts must be wrapped in paper. This Christmas, make use of other material for inventive ecological alternatives.

- ❖ Wrap in handkerchiefs or bandannas; the wrapping itself is a gift.

- ❖ Send the gift in a Christmas stocking.

- ❖ Put it in a pillow case.

- ❖ Use a cookie jar, coffee can, mug, pinata.

- ❖ Decorate a flower pot and put the gift inside.

- ❖ Put breakables in old egg cartons.

- ❖ Give edibles in a breadbox or lunchbox.

- ❖ Wrap the gift in Christmas fabric, "Hobo style," and pin shut with a corsage.

- ❖ Send it in a serviceable canvas tote bag, a wrapper that becomes a traveling companion.

- ❖ Put the gift in a handy bucket.

AN EDIBLE CONTAINER

Give Christmas cookies in a bowl made of leftover cookie dough. Gingerbread bowls are big winners.

TIE IT UP.

❖ Recycle old package bows and ribbons.

❖ If the gift is for a dog, tie it with a leash.

❖ Use cotton yarn or twine or other biodegradable material instead of plastic ribbons.

❖ Tie it with decorative shoe laces.

❖ Use hair ribbons.

❖ Tie it with an old necktie.

❖ Buckle it with belts.

❖ Recycle old scarves.

❖ Tie electrical gifts with an extention cord.

❖ Wrap sewing gifts with cloth measuring tape and use a pin cushion as a "bow".

TAG IT.

A picture, as we've heard, is worth a bunch of words. You can create a unique gift tag using a photo of the recipient.

Or if it's someone you haven't seen for some time, use both your picture and the receiver's. It'll close the gap of years and induce a warm remembrance.

Other tag ideas:

❖ Old Christmas cards

❖ Origami folded papers in Christmas shapes.

❖ Snowflakes made from cut-out paper.

HOW TO PAD THE PACKAGE...

You can prevent the contents of any package from being damaged in transit without resorting to foam padding or plastic bubble wrap. The solution is popcorn (without salt and butter!).

HOW WE PAY FOR PAPER

Manufacturing wrapping paper "costs" more than trees. To produce one ton of paper requires 261 pounds of lime, 360 pounds of salt cake, 76 pounds of soda ash, 3688 pounds of wood, 24,000 gallons of water, 28,000,000 BTUs of energy! And the manufacturing process produces 176 pounds of solid wastes, 84 pounds of air pollutants, 36 pounds of water pollutants!

Now for the good news: Using recycled paper, instead of virgin materials, reduces pollutants by 50%, lowers energy use by 70%, and water use by 60%. There is another big environmental plus: Three cubic yards of landfill is eliminated for every ton of recycled paper produced. (Three cubic yards is more than you can move using a wheelbarrow working all day!) So it pays to recycle paper and to specify "recycled" when buying paper products and printing.

Woodman, spare that tree!
Touch not a single bough!
In my youth it sheltered me,
And I'll protect it now.

—George Morris

VI.
CELEBRATING ON THE JOB

Christmas provides employers with countless opportunities to lend the environment a helping hand.

It's not unusual to spend two-thirds of our waking hours at work. So the workplace provides special opportunities to upgrade the environment. The office Christmas party is a good place to start.

The Office Party

Here are a few constructive tips for the party planner(s):

✪ **Get the right tree**. Chapter III outlined the whys and hows of having a living tree, and IV offered suggestions for decorating. These activities can be enjoyable communal functions at the office or workplace.

And before adjourning for the holidays, hold an office drawing to award the tree to the winning employee.

✪ **Celebrants' carpool**. Especially if alcohol is served at the party, it makes good sense to rent a bus, van, or limousine service to transport people home or to suburban transit stations. Short of that, arrangements should be made for a buddy system to see revelers home safely.

✪ **Rent non-disposable dinner service**. Instead of adding to the world's woes with plastic and styrofoam, rent glasses, plates, utensils and cloth napkins. If you must have disposable material, make it paper.

☆ **Buy in bulk**. Get large economy items to cut down on packaging and travel.Get giant bags of popcorn and chips, kegs of beer, large jugs of soft drinks and wine. Check with restaurant supply houses.

☆ **Buy produce loose**.Get your carrots, oranges, apples, celery, broccoli in bulk—not in small plastic bags.

☆ **Decorate with living beauty**. Order live poinsettias or other plants that can be taken home after the festivities. Other decorating thoughts:

❖ Use natural greens and pine cones.

❖ Use easy-to-recycle paper.

❖ Use timers on lights to conserve energy.

❖ Avoid using non-recyclable tinsel and foil.

☆ **Eat low on the food chain**. Eschew environmentally-costly beef, veal and pork. Go for fruits, fish, poultry, vegetables, grains, nuts. Both the earth and party-goers will be ahead.

BUSINESS GIFTS

Many companies are beginning to make environmental donations in their employees' and customers' names. Chapter III lists a number of green gift ideas, and the section following this will offer further outreach suggestions.

Another thought for employee giving is a *living* Christmas tree. If the number of employees would require a small forest of such trees, consider giving seedlings.

The Tree People, 12601 Mulholland Drive, Beverly Hills, can provide complete starter kits.

CO-WORKER GIFTS

If you give gifts to co-workers, consider these low-cost ecologically sound ideas:

☆ **A living houseplant** for their office workspace: helps clean the air and brighten the area.

☆ **A permanent ceramic coffee cup** to replace disposable, and unrecyclable materials.

✫ **A calendar, tee shirt, poster or supply of stationery** from an environmental organization that gives part of the proceeds to planting trees, or to saving rainforests or endangered species.

COMPANY CARDS

If your organization sends custom cards, print them on recycled paper. Or buy pre-printed cards from those suppliers mentioned in the last chapter.

Another way to help is to purchase Christmas cards from UNICEF or an environmental organization.

OFFICE RESOLUTIONS

Consider ending the holiday season on an "up" note by holding a staff meeting to make environmental resolutions for the New Year.

❖ Replace incandescent bulbs with florescent.

❖ Lower the thermostat a couple of degrees.

❖ Institutionalize car pooling.

❖ Establish staggered working hours.

❖ Get a copier that copies both sides.

❖ Recycle bottles, cans, paper and cardboard.

❖ Remove plastic and polystyrene from the cafeteria.

❖ Print all business forms on recycled paper

❖ Switch from white paper towels to brown.

Promoting a healthy environment is good business. Your clients/customers expect it. Public concern over the environment has never been higher; it jumped from 56% to 78% in less than three years, according to a 1990 Roper Organization report. That's the biggest change in any of the 12 national problems Roper includes in its surveys. A recent issue of *E Magazine* reports that more Americans consider themselves environmentalists than Democrats or Republicans. The mainstream is now green.

VII.
Christmas In The Community

*How your church, school, club,
professional society and other affinity groups
can celebrate constructively.*

Americans are great joiners. And most of
our associations acknowledge Christmas in one
form or the other. Perhaps this year your
group's celebration might involve giving a
helping hand to the environment.

COMMUNITY CHRISTMAS PROJECTS

✶ The Audubon Society conducts an annual, nationwide bird count between December 18 and January 1 and they need all the volunteer "counters" they can get. Come to them as a group. You don't have to be an accomplished "bird watcher" to help.

✶ Christmas caroling is a happy way for your organization to raise money for some good local environmental cause, such as a tree-planting or creek-cleaning project. You'll be more successful in high traffic locations: Shopping centers, parks, in lobbies of major office buildings, etc. Go where the shoppers are.

GIFTS TO ENJOY COME SUMMER

✶ Garden clubs and horticultural societies might form an advisory panel to provide **advice/information to local gardeners**.

✶ **Clean-up crews** are always needed to keep-up parks, schools and other public facilities. Your group could adopt a particularly forlorn site and turn it into a garden spot that would be maintained throughout the year. Or sponsor a one-time clean-up effort.

Organizing a tree-planting project is a gift any community will welcome, whether it's a one-time event or a continuing effort, or even an educational campaign. There are a lot of resource organizations ready and eager to help.

✱ **Trees For Life** (316) 263-7294 runs the "Grow-A-Tree" program, encouraging children to plant trees. It also distributes packets of material, seeds and instructions.

✱ **America The Beautiful Fund** (202)638-1649 provides technical support, small seed grants and free seeds.

✱ **Global Releaf** (202) 667-3300 helps find suitable sites.

✱ **National Arbor Day Foundation** (402) 474-5655 is a source for blue spruce seedlings.

Your County Farm Agent also can advise about what to plant, where, when and how. And usually you can obtain seedlings free or at minimal cost through state forestry departments.

CO-OP GARDEN

Another worthwhile project your organization can undertake is a cooperative garden. If your community doesn't set aside land for it, your group could consider buying and donating appropriate space.

Let anyone who's willing to do the work grow his own food. Only minimum administration is required—and the good that it does is very real.

If you have questions about how to get started, call the **American Community Gardening Association**, (213)744-4341.

ONGOING PROGRAMS YOUR GROUP CAN JOIN

Some of the worthy environmental programs your organization may wish to work with:

☆ **Center for Environmental Information**, 46 Pine St., Rochester, NY 14607. (716) 271-3550, keeps a large library, sets up conferences and seminars and publishes useful ecological information.

✬ **Adopt-A-Stream Foundation**, P.O. Box 5558, Everett, WA 98201. (206) 388-3313, invites your organization to "adopt" a stream. Your group provides for the care of the stream. Write for information on getting started.

✬ **Children of the Green Earth**, P.O. Box 95219, Seattle, WA 98145. (206) 781-0852, helps young people plant and look after forests and trees. They'll show your organization how to become active in your area.

✬ **Citizen's Clearinghouse for Hazardous Waste**, P.O. Box 3541, Arlington, VA 22216. (703) 276-7070, works with some 6,000 community groups to work for environmental sanity.

✬ **American Forestry Association**, P.O. Box 2000, Washington, DC 20013. (202) 667-3300, works to improve the health of our trees and forests. Also strives to increase awareness of the values of tree planting and conservation.

Recycling Help

Some useful reading material about community recycling projects:

☆ **Planning for Community Recycling: A Citizen's Guide to Resources.** Free. Environmental Action, 1525 New Hampshire Ave. NW, Washington, DC 20036. (202) 745-4870.

☆ **Coming Full Circle: Successful Recycling Today.** $20. The Environmental Defense Fund EDF, Park Ave. S., New York, NY 10010. (212) 505-2100.

☆ **Greenpeace Action Community Recycling Start-up Kit.** Greenpeace Action, 1436 U. St. NW, Washington, DC 20009. (202) 462-1177.

Organize A Recycling Day

You'll be primarily interested in bottles, cans and paper. But other materials are now being recycled too. Steps to set up the drive:

☆ Plan. Assign specific duties and areas. Where, when, how the collection will be made.

☆ Work with a recycling center. Be sensitive to their time demands and peak hours.

☆ Move fast. Material to be recycled shouldn't lie around. Collections should be prompt and efficient.

☆ Use the proceeds for a good ecological cause: starting gardens, planting trees, recycling education, community clean-up, etc.

> *Nothing ever goes away*
> — Barry Commoner

ADOPT A STREAM

To have healthy rivers and lakes, we must have clean streams. But more and more of these vital arteries are becoming polluted. Fertilizers and pesticides leach out of farmers' fields into our streams. Broken or leaky sewage pipes discharge waste into our streams. Erosion and litter add to the problem. Soon the fish and insects disappear and another stream is lost... unless someone comes to its rescue. A perfect project for your group. What a legacy to leave your community — a stream that runs clear and clean again, the way nature intended.

For more information and ideas contact **The Issac Walton League of America**, 1401 Wilson Blvd., Level B, Arlington, VA 22209.

"Community Action" gifts like these are so much more meaningful than just giving money. The latter is a passive, arm's length gesture, while the former involves people. You experience, first hand, a problem and become part of the solution. As a result, you adopt a proprietary connection with that solution.

When you pray for potatoes, pick up a hoe.

VIII.
THE MORE THE MERRIER
How to throw a party without putting a dent in tomorrow

The Holiday Season is for sharing, for get-togethers of all kinds. With a little care and concern, these good times won't cause violence to the environment. Here are some party-time thoughts:

FOOD COMES FIRST

Let's begin by ending our love affair with meat. Consider:

❖ Producing meat uses 10 times the water to produce equivalent energy in grain.

❖ More than 85% of the U.S. Agricultural area is used to grow meat, particularly beef and ham.

Cutting down on meat consumption saves energy, land, and other vital resources. Also, you're better off eating less meat.

Bowls of tropical fruits from Brazil are not only great party food; serving them provides a living for people in the rain forest — without putting a torch to it.

When planning party menus, think of dishes that require little or no energy to prepare:

❖ Cheese and vegetable dips

❖ Fruits, nuts, vegetables

❖ Cheese balls, crackers, popcorn

❖ No-Bake recipes like this:

Fruit-Nut Party Mix

4 cups tiny pretzels
1 cup dried tart cherries
1 cup salted mixed nuts
1 cup banana chips

Mix and store in airtight container until ready to serve. Makes 7 cups

Consider edible serving containers: A hollowed-out bread loaf for dip or cheese; a pumpkin for soup; a red pepper for herbs.

HEARTWARMING DRINKS

Some parties adapt the traditional Wassail Bowl to alcohol-free drinks. You can serve a thick, rich-tasting nog that goes light on the calories using low-fat milk. Hold the rum and brandy.

Hot chocolate with cinnamon and gobs of whipped cream rarely fails to please-goers of all ages.

Hot mulled cider is another crowd-pleaser. Use whole allspice and dried bits of orange peel with the heated cider.

Shop Smart

❖ Use cloth instead of paper napkins and towels

❖ Rent or borrow infrequently used items: punch bowls, chafing dishes, etc.

❖ Support the small farmer: Shop at Farmer's Markets when possible.

❖ Buy eggs in cardboard containers instead of styrofoam.

❖ Go for the large economy sizes for things that won't spoil: Rice, soap, sugar, grains, nuts, dried fruits, pet food. You'll save time, gasoline, money — and reduce garbage.

❖ Buy biodegradable soaps.

❖ Bring your own tote bag, or cardboard boxes to haul home your purchases.

❖ And remember: No plastic containers/ bags, no aerosol sprays, no non-returnable bottles.

AFTER THE PARTY

❖ Recycle aluminum cans.

❖ Rinse and reuse aluminum foil.

❖ Wash and reuse glass jars.

❖ Stick to biodegradable packages.

❖ Reuse cardboard boxes.

❖ Recycle magazines and papers.

❖ Reuse gift paper.

❖ Use garbage cans, not bags.

All these party ideas have one thing in common: they're group-oriented, participatory, calculated to bring people together in the Spirit of Christmas. And the essence of that Spirit is:

PEACE ON EARTH

There is no greater gift we can make to the environment. For only the peaceful can live in harmony with Nature.

IX
BLESSED ARE THE CHILDREN

Christmas belongs to the children.

To be sure, children can raise the noise level several decibels. Their fingerprints are everywhere. Candy disappears as if by magic. Your decorations, your tree, wrapping, gifts, music, food…everything is imprinted with their presence. They cheerily contribute their special chaos.

Where there are children, there are stockings hanging from the mantel and sticky things to eat.

Lets Talk Food

Here are some ideas for things to serve at a kids' party that are good for both the children and the earth:

☆ **Apple cide**r. Buy it by the gallon to cut down on containers.

☆ **Rainforest crunch, popcorn, home-made cookies, oranges, apples.**

☆ **Finger foods** like carrot sticks, celery, little sandwiches. Stuff that won't require plastic plates.

☆ **Candy bought in bulk** to avoid plastic wrappers.

☆ **Make-it-yourself goodies**: caramel apples, taffy, brownies, fudge.

And For Party Favors:

☆ **Seedlings**, like a tiny fir tree that can be taken home and planted.

☆ **Tickets** to a local nature museum, zoo, or aquarium.

☆ **Personalized mug** or cup to take home — instead of throw-away cups.

☆ **Party decorations to take home** after the ball: wind socks, kites, banners, place settings with the guest's picture. Avoid unrecyclable mylar balloons.

'TIS MORE BLESSED...

In the true spirit of Christmas, organize activities to help others:

☆ Ask each child to bring a toy to be donated to a children's shelter.

☆ Organize a children's work party to make new Christmas cards from recycled materials to donate to hospitals, old folks' homes, hospices.

☆ Give the youngsters a living tree to decorate and donate to a deserving charity.

☆ Form a children's chorus to go caroling for people and places in need of Holiday cheering-up.

Games Children Play

If the weather permits, help the children organize a recycling scavenger hunt, with prizes for the most or biggest recycling items brought back for the local recycling center.

And if the weather is strictly stay-inside, rent a nature VCR, such as Never Cry Wolf, or a National Geographic Special or Jacques Cousteau program.

Better yet, invite a live story-teller. For example, invite the help of a park ranger, naturalist, or other knowledgeable ecologist to spin yarns about the enthralling world of nature. It's an environmental alternative to Santa.

Party Popper

Here's a good way to recycle wrapping or tissue scraps into easy-to-make party favors.

Assemble paper, glue, string, small candy or other goodies and a toilet tissue roll. Cut the toilet paper tube in half and let the kids do the rest:

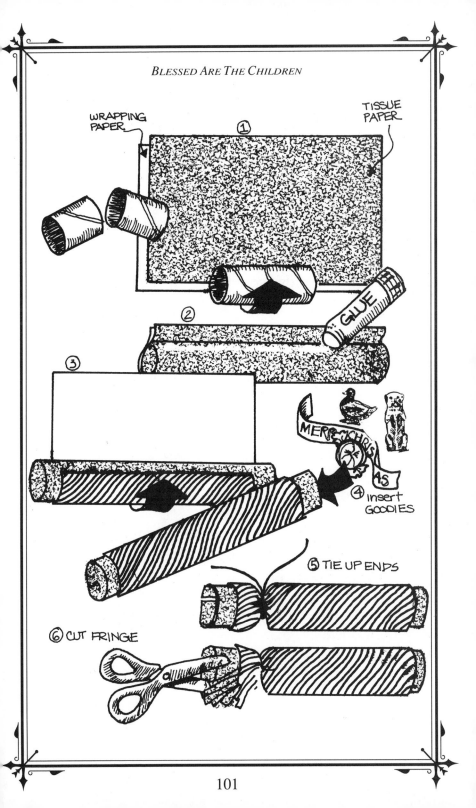

WRAPPING PAPER

TISSUE PAPER

① ② ③

GLUE

MERRY CHRISTMAS

④ insert GOODIES

⑤ TIE UP ENDS

⑥ CUT FRINGE

SANTA'S WISH LIST

If Santa does come to the party, he turns the tables on the children after hearing "What I want for Christmas" lists by giving them *his* wish list: things they can do to make their world better.

☆ The kids would pick up neighborhood litter.

☆ They would plant a garden.

☆ They would give old toys to needy children.

☆ They wouldn't litter.

☆ They would take care of their possessions so they wouldn't become trash.

☆ They would check for dripping faucets at home. They would see that lights and TV are turned off at night.

☆ They wouldn't leave the refrigerator door open.

☆ They would respect all growing things.

MAKING IT SAFE

Christmas presents a host of opportunities for little party-goers to get in harm's way. Here are some common-sense ways to see that they survive the festivities unscathed:

✯ Before the party, check the condition of smoke alarms, fire extinguishers, just in case...

✯ Be sure your Christmas tree is solidly anchored, so excited young hands can't pull the glittering symbol on top of them.

✯ Keep an eye on the tiny guests if there are presents like pull toys or toy phones with cords that could strangle.

✯ Beware of balloons. When they have popped, children can choke on the remains.

✯ Keep plastic wrap, styrofoam chips or other packing material away, too. It can get lodged in the toddler's throat.

✯ Make sure that extension cords are where children can't get at them.

✯ Watch the kids around ribbons and other wrapping material that could choke them.

WATCH OUT FOR TOXIC PLANTS

It is not generally known that a lot of the lovely green and growing things that are celebrated and given at Christmastime have troublesome toxic properties.

That does not mean the plants should be avoided. It *does* mean we should be cautious with them around children.

The following plants may cause serious illness. Call a doctor or local Poison Hotline at once if exposure is suspected:

❖ Azalea (*Rhododendron occidentalle*)

❖ Christmas Rose (*Helleborus niger*)

❖ Chrysanthemum

❖ Laurel, English (*Prunus laurocerasus*)

❖ Mistletoe, Amer. (*Phoradendon flavescens*)

❖ Mistletoe, European (*Viscum album*)

❖ Toyon leaves (*Heteromeles arbulifolia*)

These plants can cause stomach cramping, breathing difficutlties, burning to the mouth if eaten, or a rash if contacted on the skin:

❖ Amaryllis, Common (*Hippeastrum*)

❖ Anthurium

❖ Boston Ivy (*Parthenocissus tricuspidata*)

❖ Box, Boxwood (*Buxus*)

❖ English Ivy (*Hedera helix*)

❖ Glacier Ivy (*Hedera glacier*)

❖ Holly berry (*Ilex aquifolium*)

❖ Ivy, Amer. (*Parthenocissus quinoquefolia*)

❖ Narciussus

❖ Parlor Ivy (*Philodendron cordatum*)

❖ Poinsettia (*Euphorbia pulcherrima*)

❖ Pyracantha berry, thorn

❖ Ripple Ivy (*Hedera helix 'ripple'*)

❖ Yew (*Taxus*)

A couple of general rules:

☆ Do not asume a plant is safe simply because birds or animals eat it.

☆ Keep poisonous plant bulbs and seeds away from youngsters.

IT'S THEIR PARTY

But with all the potential problems and pitfalls, a Christmas party for the children is an enriching experience.

The guiding hand of parents, though essential, is best applied with a minimum of visibilty. After all, it's *their* party.

And the guiding principle should be the spirit of the season: Enjoy!

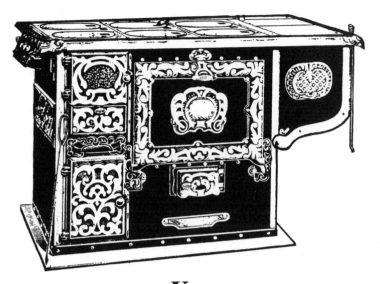

X.
KITCHEN CONSERVATION

Tips on saving time, money and energy preparing the Christmas feast.

Kitchens are busy places during the Holidays. So many of the gifts and decorations mentioned earlier are made here. Long before it's time to prepare Christmas Dinner, a stream of friends and relatives comes dropping in, most of them gravitating to the kitchen.

No wonder your December gas and electric bill always is a shocker. Your range is working overtime. The oven's always occupied. The refrigerator door is seldom closed. The tap runs hot day and night. And the kitchen's lights are the last to be shut off.

> *Sing a song of mincemeat, currants, raisins, spice, apples, sugar, nutmeg, everythings that's nice, stir it with a ladle, wish a lovely wish, drop it in the middle of your well-filled dish, stir again for good luck, pack it all away tied in little jars and pots until Christmas Day.*
>
> —Elizabeth Gould

First, make sure your appliances are functioning efficiently. **Test the thermostat in your oven. Check the reflectors under your stove-top burners.** One-third of the energy used for stovetop cooking is wasted because reflectors don't reflect! Make sure yours are bright and shiny. If they won't shine, replace. Or cover with foil shaped to fit. You'll be money ahead.

And make every effort to use the right size pots and pans. The bigger the container, the more energy is used to heat the contents. Flat-bottoms are more efficient for electric and smooth cook-tops.

Check the oven door seal. Clean, and if you find any tears or gaps, repair or replace. If you have a gas oven, the pilot light should be a blue, cone-shaped flame. If it's yellow or a jumpy blue, you're wasting gas. Ask your power company to make adjustments.

By using ceramic baking dishes you can lower oven temperatures 25%.

Dust the condenser coils behind or under your refrigerator and check the door seal. This is the most energy-hungry appliance in the kitchen. If your temperature is set below 40° and 42°, redial for dollars! (Freezers should be set between 0° and 5°.)

Letting warm leftovers cool before refrigerating is a simple and effective energy-saving habit.

Whatever you do, don't cook with the oven door open. There is no more wasteful practice! And resist peeking. Every time you open the oven door, you waste 25 to 50 degrees, or more.

Don't overdo the pre-heating. 10 minutes is plenty. And remember, pre-heating is unnecessary for broiling.

If you own a microwave oven, use it whenever possible. It uses about 50% less energy than your stove's oven. (If you don't own a microwave, put that on the top of your Christmas Wish List.)

If a lot of water goes down the drain waiting for the sink tap to run hot, keep a jug handy to catch it. If you don't use it to drink or cook with, you can use this supply for watering plants.

Kitchen lights burn late and long during winter, especially around the Holidays. By substituting the new screw-in compact flourescent bulbs for incandescent, you'll use 75% less energy. For instant ignition and to eliminate flickering and buzzing, obtain the new electronic ballast model. Those new fluorescent lights also keep a half-ton of CO_2 out of the atmosphere over the life of the bulb (which is 10 times longer than incandescent!).

XI.
HAPPY NEW YEAR!
Making 1992 cleaner and greener.

A *happy, healthy* New Year, as well as a *prosperous* one, depends very much on the quality of the environment: locally, regionally, globally.

The environmental conditions that greet us next year will have been determined by the actions or inaction of the nine billion humans who have inhabited this planet to date, yourself included.

So what can one person like yourself do in one year to undo the damage done over thousands of years by billions of people? **Plenty.**

> *Nobody made a greater mistake*
> *than he who did nothing because*
> *he could only do a little.*
> —Edmund Burke

The great Ghandi had this to say about individual effort: "Your individual actions may seem unimportant, but it is absolutely essential you do them."

LITTLE THINGS MEAN A LOT

It's easy to ignore all the do's and don'ts in books like this. Each one seems but a trifle — a plastic bag here, an old tin can there. What does one leaky faucet amount to when an alfalfa field requires thousands of gallons of water every week? But when millions mind the trifles, the effect is tremendous! A city full of litter would come miraculously clean if each person in it didn't litter.

Most environmental damage has been wrought in the last 150 years of man's reign. The effects are correctible in even a shorter time frame. Rivers and streams flowing thick with chemical wastes and effluent can be made to run pure again in less than a decade.

England's Thames River, for example, went from being a cesspool to a Salmon-run river in less than 10 years. The soot and grime that once coated city buildings in many U.K. coal-producing regions is now a thing of the past.

> *Pollution is nothing but the resources we're not harvesting.*
> —*R. Buckminster Fuller*

We can clear up the air quality in places like the Los Angeles basin, stop acid rain from denuding Eastern forests and prevent any further degrading of the protective ozone layer before the end of this decade — if we are willing to take the trouble and spend the money. The technology is waiting for the will!

GREEN RESOLUTIONS FOR THE NEW YEAR

Now is the time to consider a commitment in the form of a Green Resolution.

❖ Eat at the bottom of the food chain.

❖ Compost whenever possible.

❖ Switch from incandescent lights to fluorescent.

❖ Plant at least one tree.

❖ Use only cloth cleaning towels.

❖ Turn off the shower while you soap.

❖ Install water-saving devices in your toilet and shower.

❖ Walk or bicycle at least one car errand weekly.

❖ Use re-usable cloth bags to shop.

❖ Get a permanent coffee cup for the job.

❖ Use biodegradable laundry soap, not detergents.

❖ Turn down the thermostat at night.

❖ Recycle your bottles, cans, papers.

❖ Think—really think—about the future of our planet.

❖ Buy recycled products (those with a Green Seal).

❖ Cut down on pesticides.

❖ Switch to cloth diapers.

❖ Celebrate and love your Earth.

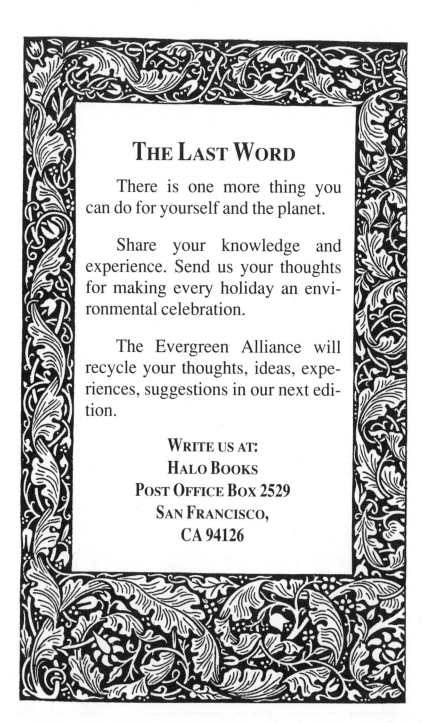

The Last Word

There is one more thing you can do for yourself and the planet.

Share your knowledge and experience. Send us your thoughts for making every holiday an environmental celebration.

The Evergreen Alliance will recycle your thoughts, ideas, experiences, suggestions in our next edition.

Write us at:
Halo Books
Post Office Box 2529
San Francisco,
CA 94126